WHY SHOULD I EAT THIS CARROT?

✦ and other questions about healthy eating ✦

Louise Spilsbury

Heinemann Library
Chicago, Illinois

© 2003 Heinemann Library,
a division of Reed Elsevier Inc.
Chicago, Illinois

Customer Service 888-454-2279

Visit our website at www.heinemannlibrary.com

Designed by David Poole and Tokay Interactive Ltd
Illustrations by Kamae Design Ltd
Originated by Ambassador Litho Ltd
Printed in China by Wing King Tong

07 06 05 04 03
10 9 8 7 6 5 4 3 2 1

Library of Congress Cataloging-in-Publication Data
Spilsbury, Louise.
  Why should I eat this carrot? and other questions about healthy eating / Louise Spilsbury.
     v. cm. -- (Body matters)
Includes bibliographical references and index.
Contents: Why is healthy eating important? -- How does my body turn food into energy? -- Why should I drink water? -- Why do athletes eat pasta? -- Why is brown bread better than white? -- Are smoothies good for you? -- Why should I eat this carrot? -- What is so bad about fat? -- Why wash fruit before eating it? -- What makes a healthy snack? -- Food pyramid.
ISBN 1-4034-4680-6 (HC)
 1. Nutrition--Juvenile literature. 2. Metabolism--Juvenile literature. [1. Nutrition. 2. Food habits. 3. Metabolism. 4. Health.]
I. Title. II. Series.
  RA784.S658 2003
  613.2--dc21

                                        2003004980

Acknowledgments
The author and publishers are grateful to the following for permission to reproduce copyright material: pp. 4, 5, 8, 12, 18, 22 Getty Images; p. 6 Corbis/Dennis M. Gottlieb; p. 9 Corbis/ Lynda Richardson; p. 10 Corbis/Tom Stewart; p. 11 Corbis/S. Carmona; p. 13 Corbis Images/Peter Beck; p. 14 Photodisc; pp. 15, 16 Trevor Clifford; p. 17 Corbis/Laura Dwight; pp. 19, 24 Trevor Clifford; p. 20 Chris Honeywell; p. 21 Corbis/Reed Kaestner; pp. 23, 25, 27 Tudor Photography; p. 26 Liz Eddison; p. 28 Corbis/Charles Gupton.

Cover photograph by Tudor Photography.

Some words are shown in bold, **like this.** You can find out what they mean by looking in the glossary.

CONTENTS

WHY IS HEALTHY EATING IMPORTANT?

You may have heard the old saying "You are what you eat." This may sound like nonsense, but it is true. The food you eat provides your body with the **energy** it needs to live and with the materials it needs to grow and to repair parts that are worn out or damaged.

Staying alive

Our bodies are made up of millions of tiny **cells.** These are so small that you can see them only through a microscope. Up to when you are about eighteen years old, your body makes new cells so that you can grow. When you are an adult, your body continues to make new cells to replace old or damaged ones. The energy to make and repair body cells comes from the food you eat. To build a strong and healthy body, you need to eat healthy kinds of food.

You need energy for everything you do—from sleeping to skateboarding.

What are nutrients?

The parts of food your body uses for growth and energy are called **nutrients.** You cannot see or taste them, but you need a variety of nutrients for your body to work properly and to stay healthy. There are five main kinds of nutrients— **proteins, fats, minerals, vitamins,** and **carbohydrates.** To be healthy, you also need to drink water and eat **fiber.** You will find out more about all of these types of nutrients in this book.

We need to eat a healthy mixture of different foods because different nutrients help your body in different ways.

WHAT IS A DIET?

When you hear people say that they are on a diet, what they really mean is that they are on a diet to lose weight. In fact, your diet is basically the food you eat every day. A balanced diet means eating the foods that make your body healthy.

HOW DOES MY BODY TURN FOOD INTO ENERGY?

Food contains all the nutrients your body needs to live and grow, but digestion is needed to break food into separate particles that your body can use.

The food on your plate is no good to your body as it is. To use food, your body has to break it down into pieces so tiny they can get into your blood. This process is called **digestion.**

Digesting food

Your body starts to digest food as soon as you put it into your mouth. Your teeth chew the food into smaller pieces and mix it with saliva (spit) to make it soft. Then your tongue pushes the mashed-up food into your throat so that you can swallow it. **Muscles** inside the esophagus—a long tube leading down from your throat—move the food down to your stomach.

Food stays in your stomach for about five hours. Here, special juices break the pieces of food into even smaller pieces. When these move into the small intestine, they are mixed with more digestive juices until they become so small that they can pass into your blood.

Nutrients in the blood

Your blood is like a fleet of delivery trucks that travel around your body through a network of tubes called blood vessels. Your blood brings **nutrients** from the digested food to the different kinds of **cells** all over your body. The cells use this **energy** to divide and increase in number so that you can grow. They also use energy to repair themselves when they are damaged.

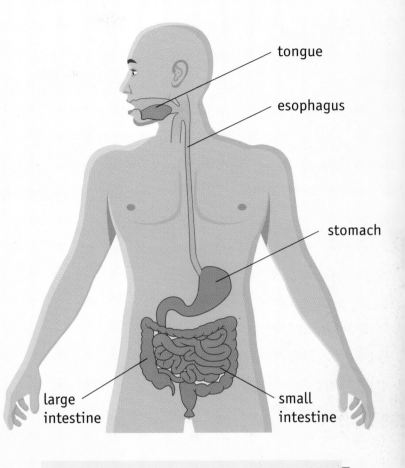

tongue

esophagus

stomach

large intestine

small intestine

Food takes about a day to pass through your **digestive system.** Waste material moves from the small intestine to the large intestine. This waste passes out of your body when you go to the bathroom.

WHY SHOULD I DRINK WATER?

Water is the most important **nutrient** of all. Your body can survive for weeks without food but only a few days without water. In fact, you are made up mostly of water! Your body can work properly only if you keep your water level up.

Water in your body

All of the fluids in your body contain water. One of these, the blood, is your body's transport system, carrying nutrients and **oxygen** to parts that need them and taking away waste. Water keeps body parts, such as **joints,** lubricated (moving freely). Watery saliva moves food through your **digestive system.** Water also forms a cushion over important parts, such as your brain, to protect them from bumps.

Topping up your water

You lose lots of water every day—through sweating, urination, and other things your body does—and you need to take in more water than you lose. You should drink about six glasses of water a day. You can get some of the water you need from foods that contain lots of water, such as fruit, vegetables, and soup, but do not substitute other drinks, such as soda, for water. Pure water is the best possible drink to keep your body healthy.

Nine-tenths of the weight of some fruit and vegetables, such as melon or cucumber, is water.

WHAT IS DEHYDRATION?

Dehydration is when your body has lost more water than it has taken in. Sometimes people get dehydrated when they are sick or because they do not drink enough water when it is hot and they are sweating. It is very unhealthy to get dehydrated, so drink water often—don't wait until you feel thirsty.

9

WHY DO ATHLETES EAT PASTA?

Some athletes eat pasta and foods such as bread, grains, and potatoes when they are training because these foods give them **energy.** They are called **carbohydrates.** Most people do not need to eat lots of carbohydrates before a race or game, but you should always try to make carbohydrates the main part of every meal.

Carbohydrates for energy

When you **digest** your food, most of it is broken down into glucose, a kind of sugar. The glucose moves into your blood. The blood carries the glucose and **oxygen** all over your body. The glucose and oxygen are mixed inside the body's **cells.** There, they react together and release energy.

Carbohydrates are the body's fuel— they are **nutrients** that give you the energy you need to beat your friend at chess or to ride your bike.

Energy for later

Some of the glucose that your body does not use right away is stored in cells in your **liver** and **muscles** in a form called glycogen. If there is too much glycogen to store in your liver and muscle cells, the rest is stored as body fat.

Later on, your body can use these glycogen stores for energy, just as a car uses gasoline from its fuel tank. If you do a short burst of exercise, such as running for a bus, your body uses the glycogen for energy. If you do a lot of exercise for a longer time, perhaps when you play in a soccer game or take the dog for a walk, your body uses up some of your fat store for energy.

Marathon runners have to race 26 miles (nearly 42 kilometers) without a lunch break, so they know how important carbohydrates are for giving the body energy that lasts.

11

Kinds of carbohydrates

There are two kinds of **carbohydrates**—simple and complex. Simple carbohydrates are those that your body can **digest** and absorb into the blood simply and quickly. Sugar is a simple carbohydrate, and you find it in cakes, cookies, and other sweet foods. Many fruits contain a kind of sugar, too. Fruits are a lot better for you because they also contain other healthy **nutrients.**

Complex carbohydrates take longer to travel through your body's **digestive system** because they are trickier to digest. For this reason, they release **energy** more slowly and over a longer period of time. You find complex carbohydrates in bread, grains, noodles, potatoes, and many other varieties of vegetables. These are sometimes called starchy foods.

Complex carbohydrates, such as pasta, are better for you than simple carbohydrates. Along with giving you lots of slow-release energy, they also contain **fat** and **fiber,** to help you be healthy.

Staple foods

Staple foods are those that people eat a lot of because they grow well in their country. For example, rice is a staple food in China. Staple foods are always carbohydrates, and they are called staple—meaning basic and necessary—because people need them to live. You should eat a variety of carbohydrates and try to make them a staple part of your diet. Eat some at every meal and also as snacks sometimes.

In Central America, corn is a staple food, because it is the main carbohydrate that people eat.

WHAT ARE CALORIES?

Calories are a measure of how much energy a food can supply to your body. At your age, you need about 2,400 calories every day because your body uses up a lot of energy to keep you going and growing. Carbohydrates contain useful calories—two slices of bread or one banana each give you about 100 calories.

13

WHY IS WHEAT BREAD BETTER THAN WHITE?

Bread is made using flour, and flour is made from crushed grains (seeds) of wheat. White flour is made from the inside of the grain. Whole-wheat flour is made from the whole grain, including the skin around the seed, called bran. Bran contains **fiber,** which helps keep your body healthy.

To make white bread, the bran is removed from the seeds that grow on wheat plants like these. Wheat bread still has this nutritious outer layer.

Lots of fiber

All plant foods contain fiber—little thin strands like threads. You can see them easily in plant foods, such as celery. The problem is that many of the foods we eat are processed, meaning that they are treated and changed before they are packaged and sold in stores. Processing often removes fiber. So to be healthy, you should eat more fresh fruit and vegetables. Try to eat five servings every day.

Fiber for health

Fiber is not a **nutrient.** In fact, it is a part of food that we cannot **digest** at all. As it passes through our bodies, however, it helps our **digestive system** work properly. Fiber soaks up water like a sponge, making waste material from your food softer. This means that it passes through the large intestine and out of your body more quickly. This is good because it is unhealthy to have food waste in your body for too long.

SOME FIBER-RICH FOODS

These foods contain lots of fiber:
- fresh and dried fruit, such as bananas and apricots
- oatmeal
- vegetables, such as broccoli and potatoes
- beans, such as baked beans
- nuts and seeds, such as sunflower seeds and peanuts.

Eating fiber-rich foods like these prevents you from becoming constipated. Constipation is when the **feces** becomes too dry and hard to pass easily out of the body.

15

ARE SMOOTHIES GOOD FOR YOU?

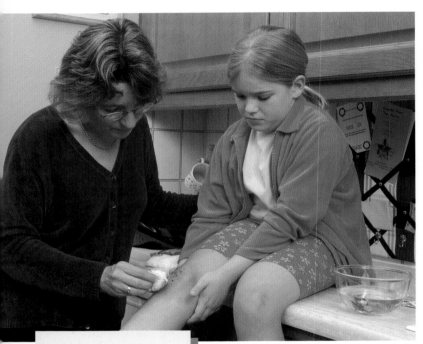

When you fall and hurt yourself, protein helps your cuts and scrapes heal.

Smoothies made from milk and fresh fruit are good for you—not just because they taste good, but also because they are a good source of **protein.** Milk and other dairy products, such as cheese, are rich in protein. Protein is an important **nutrient** that everyone needs to build a healthy body.

Protein—the body builder

Protein is often called the body builder because it is the main ingredient in all of your body parts, including your **muscles,** skin, and **liver.** You also need protein to replace or repair parts when they are worn out or damaged and to make hemoglobin, the part of your blood that carries vital **oxygen** around your body. Protein has another important job. It makes antibodies, which are special **cells** that attack **infections** that can make you ill.

What is protein?

Protein is not just a single substance—it is made up of many smaller parts called amino acids. When you **digest** protein foods, your body breaks them down into these separate parts. Your body uses the different amino acids like building blocks. It puts them together again in different combinations to build themany cells that form the different parts of your body.

Your body uses protein to build body parts, but whether it makes hair or fingers depends on which amino acids the protein contains. Amino acids are the building blocks of protein.

Your body can make some of the amino acids you need by using substances that are already stored inside your body. The other amino acids that you need—called essential amino acids— can get into your body only from protein foods. For this reason, it is very important to eat some protein foods every day.

WHAT IF I AM A VEGETARIAN?

If you are a vegetarian, you do not eat meat. So how do you get all the protein you need when plant foods do not contain all the essential amino acids? Different kinds of plant foods have different amino acids, so the trick is to mix them together to be healthy.

Protein foods

There is some **protein** in all foods. Animal foods that are rich in protein include meat, fish, and dairy products, such as cheese. Plant foods that contain protein include beans, nuts, and grains. Animal proteins contain almost all of the essential amino acids a body needs. Many plant foods, however, are low in or lack certain essential amino acids.

If you are a vegetarian, it is easy to mix different proteins. When you eat pizza, you are combining grains and a dairy product.

How much protein should I eat?

Although proteins are vitally important to your health, you do not need to eat a huge amount of them. In fact, many protein foods also contain **fats,** so it is unhealthy to eat more than you need. If you eat a protein food or a mix of protein foods as part of your main meals twice a day, and perhaps include them in your snacks sometimes, you should get all you need.

The important thing is to eat some foods with protein in them every day. Your body cannot store proteins, so you need to keep filling yourself up with these **nutrients.**

When choosing protein foods, do not think about only how much protein they have. Peanut butter is a good protein choice, but it is less healthy for you if it has lots of added sugar and salt.

WHY SHOULD I EAT THIS CARROT?

If you want to watch fireworks at night or enjoy a rainbow, eat your carrots! Carrots contain **vitamin** A—a **nutrient** that helps your eyes see well in the dark and tell the difference between colors. Vitamin A is just one of the vitamins your body needs to be healthy.

Different kinds of vitamins

There are two kinds of vitamins—fat-soluble and water-soluble. Vitamins A, D, E, and K are fat-soluble because your body stores them in body fat (and in your **liver**). Vitamin C and the different B vitamins are water-soluble because they become part of the water that makes up your blood. If they are not used up as they travel around your body in your blood, they pass out of your body when you urinate.

Because your body cannot store water-soluble vitamins, you need to eat food that contains them every day. Oranges contain a lot of vitamin C, a water-soluble vitamin.

VITAL VITAMINS

This list tells you the main vitamins you need, how they help you, and where to find them.

vitamin A Helps with eyesight, growth, and healthy skin. Found in fruits, vegetables, and milk.

B vitamins Help you make **energy** and healthy blood **cells**. Found in fish, meats, eggs, beans, bread, and vegetables.

vitamin C Gives you healthy gums and teeth, builds strong **muscles** and bones, and helps you fight **infections** and heal wounds. Found in fruits and many vegetables.

vitamin D Helps you build strong bones and teeth and absorb a nutrient called **calcium**. Found in milk, fish, eggs, and nuts.

vitamin E Protects your body's **tissues** and helps you use other vitamins properly. Found in vegetable oils, green vegetables, and nuts.

vitamin K Helps your blood clot when you are cut. Found in dark green vegetables and cheese.

What are minerals?

You often hear **vitamins** linked with another **nutrient—minerals.** Like vitamins, minerals are vital for your health, and you need only small amounts of them. Two important minerals are calcium and iron.

Calcium

Calcium is especially important for building strong bones and teeth. It also helps your **muscles** and nerves work properly. You get the calcium you need from milk and other dairy products, such as yogurt and cheese, and from leafy green vegetables, such as cabbage.

If you get low on iron, you feel tired and lacking in **energy.** When people do not have enough iron for a long time, they get an illness called **anemia.**

Iron

Your body needs iron to help your blood carry the **oxygen** around your body. Your body parts need oxygen to make energy from your food. Meats, fish, raisins, and cereals are good sources of iron.

Other minerals

Your body needs tiny amounts of many different minerals with interesting-sounding names, such as zinc, magnesium, and phosphorous. You often see these listed on food packaging. But don't worry—you do not have to read lots of labels to check that you are getting all the minerals you need. Just eat a healthy diet with different kinds of food.

Salt is another important mineral, but you should get enough from your food. Too much salt is bad for you, so there is no need to add extra to your food.

DO I NEED VITAMIN AND MINERAL PILLS?

If you eat a wide range of foods, you get all the vitamins and minerals you need. Many people who take pills with extra nutrients—called supplements—probably don't need them. It shouldn't do them any harm, though, because the body gets rid of any nutrients it does not use.

WHAT IS SO BAD ABOUT FAT?

People are warned not to eat too many fatty foods because they contain a lot of **calories.** Your body can use only so many calories at a time, so it stores the rest as body fat. This makes some people overweight. Overweight people are more likely to suffer from health problems when they are older, such as heart disease and **diabetes.**

Is some fat good for me?

It is very important to get some fat from the foods you eat. Your body uses **fat** to give you **energy,** and many of your **cells** need fat to form properly. Having a thin layer of body fat around you keeps your body warm and cushions your insides from bumps.

No food type is really bad for you —what counts is how often you eat it and what else you eat. Some fats, such as butter, are fine in small amounts and even contain some **vitamins.**

Which foods contain fat?

There are two main kinds of fat—saturated and unsaturated. Saturated fats are found in red meats and dairy products. Unsaturated fats are found in fish and white meats, such as chicken, and in plant parts or products, such as avocados and olive oil. Unsaturated fats are slightly healthier than saturated fats, but you should not eat too much of either.

FAT-BUSTING TIPS

Here are some ways you can avoid eating too much fat:

- eat grilled, steamed, microwaved, or stir-fried food instead of food that has been roasted or fried in oil
- eat yogurt or fruit for dessert instead of cookies or cake
- eat baked potatoes rather than fries or potato chips
- eat fish or chicken sometimes instead of beef.

This girl is enjoying a salmon and cream cheese bagel. The fat in oily fish, such as salmon, is good for you. It helps your blood flow around your body more easily.

WHY WASH FRUIT BEFORE EATING IT?

Washing or scrubbing fruits and vegetables well before you eat them is better than peeling them because the most nutritious part is just below the surface of their skin!

Many farms use artificial chemicals to help crops grow bigger. They also use chemicals to kill pests that try to eat food plants while they are growing. Often these chemicals stay on the skin of fruits and vegetables when they get to the stores. That is why it is best to wash or peel fresh foods to get rid of any chemicals before you eat them.

What are organic foods?

Organic farms grow crops and raise animals without using artificial chemicals. Instead, organic farmers use compost and manure from farm animals to feed the land, and they use other plants and insects to control pests. Some people believe that organic food is safer to eat than food that is grown using chemicals.

Always keep pets and flies away from food because they can spread germs.

Keeping food clean and fresh

The food you eat must be clean and fresh. Otherwise it can make you ill. Wash your hands before eating or preparing food to stop germs from getting onto your food. Store food properly, according to the instructions on labels. **Bacteria** from raw foods, such as meat, can spread to cooked foods easily, so keep them apart in the fridge. Do not eat food that has gone bad. This means that bacteria are growing on it, and some bacteria can make you ill.

WHAT ARE GM FOODS?

GM stands for "genetically modified." GM foods come from plants that scientists have changed by adding or taking away certain **genes.** Some people avoid GM foods because they are not sure what effects these changes to the plants could have on people's health.

WHAT MAKES A HEALTHY SNACK?

IDEAS FOR HEALTHY SNACKS

Why not try pretzels, unbuttered popcorn, fruit, fruit smoothies, breadsticks, crackers, bagels, rice cakes, fruit or cereal bars, carrot or celery sticks, or a bowl of whole-wheat cereal without added sugar?

Your body is growing fast, and it is natural to want a snack sometimes. Your body can use sweet and fatty foods, such as cookies and chips, to make **energy** quickly, but the energy lasts only a short time. Also, these foods have few **nutrients.** Complex **carbohydrates,** such as cereals or bread, take longer to **digest** and give you energy for longer. These and other healthy snacks, such as fruit, also give your body some of the **vitamins, minerals,** and **fiber** it needs.

It is fine to eat sweet or fatty snacks sometimes, but try to eat healthy snacks more often.

HEALTHY EATING

The food pyramid is an easy way to see the variety and amount of foods that make up a healthy diet. You should eat 6 to 11 servings a day from the grain group at the bottom of the pyramid. Eat 2 to 4 servings of fruits and 3 to 5 servings of vegetables a day. Eat 2 to 3 servings from the milk group and 2 to 3 servings from the meat group. Do not eat too many fats and sweets, which are at the top of the pyramid.

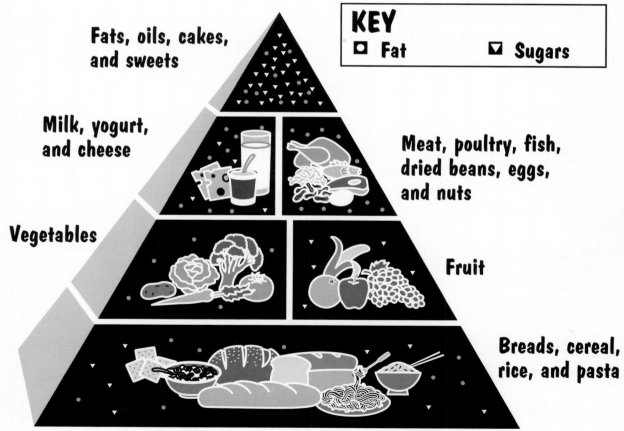

Source: U.S. Department of Agriculture/U.S. Department of Health and Human Services

GLOSSARY

anemia   illness that makes you feel weak and tired. It is caused by a lack of iron in the blood.

bacteria   tiny living things that can cause disease

calcium   nutrient that helps build strong bones and teeth

calorie   measure of the energy value of food

carbohydrate   nutrient in food that gives you energy

cell   smallest building block of living things

diabetes   disease that makes people unable to use food to make the energy their body needs

digest   way the body breaks down the food you eat

digestive system   parts of the body that digest food

energy   power that allows living things to do everything they need to live and grow

fat   substance found in food that is naturally oily or greasy

feces   solid waste produced by the body

fiber   part of plant foods, such as vegetables and fruits, that the body cannot digest

genes   information in all living things that determines the way they are

infection   kind of disease that can be caught by other people

joint   place where two bones join

liver organ in the body that stores nutrients from the blood and breaks down waste

mineral chemical found in rocks and soil. Similar substances found in foods are needed by your body.

muscle bunch of fibers that move a part of your body

nutrient kind of chemical found in food that you need to be healthy

oxygen gas in the air that you need to live

protein substance in some of the foods you eat that your body can use to build or repair body parts

tissues groups of cells connected together

vitamin substance found in food that your body needs to be healthy

FURTHER READING

Gregson, Susan R. *Healthy Eating*. Mankato, Minn.: Capstone, 2000.

Sommers, Michael A. *Everything You Need to Know About Looking and Feeling Your Best: A Guide for Guys*. New York: Rosen, 2000.

Sommers, Michael A. *Everything You Need to Know About Looking and Feeling Your Best: A Guide for Girls*. New York: Rosen, 2000.

INDEX